The Secrets to the Profitable Startup

Copyright

Title book: The Secrets to the Profitable Startup

Author book: Nuno Arroteia, Bibek Bhatta

First Published: 2018

ISBN 9781070937618

© 2018, Startup Finance Limited

Startup Finance Limited

1 Lilybank Terrace

Dundee, DD4 6BQ, United Kingdom

Web: www.startup-finance.co.uk

E-mail: esales@startup-finance.co.uk

Table of Contents

Introduction

This book is intended to be a quick and useful guide to analyse the profitability of any business venture. It establishes a methodology centred on the break-even analysis to examine a business activity.

Moreover, it also covers introductory aspects which are related to the break-even analysis such as pricing, budgeting and investment appraisal.

Profitability is not always a result of revenues. It is of course significant to generate sales, but businesses should also be analysed on how the balance between revenues and costs impacts on the profits.

The examples provided in this book are designed to quickly and effectively introduce these key concepts so that the readers can immediately apply them to any project related to starting or expanding a business.

As the book is written in a way that discusses the fundamentals straightaway, it may not be suitable for someone expecting to gain an in-depth knowledge of aspects related to business finance and accounting.

This is also not an academic book. Despite using insights both from the authors' business experience and proven academic research, it is written without adopting the formality and rigidity of academic writing.

Therefore, its reduced size should fit the needs of speed and effectiveness that most entrepreneurs nowadays require.

Adequate knowledge about managing costs is a powerful tool to support firms' sustainability in the case of either revenues stagnation or growth.

Therefore, this book analyses various pathways to success and discusses the relevant issues from the perspective of how costs should be managed to maximise the profitability of a business.

The topics do not cover aspects such as increasing revenues, but instead, focus on how managing costs are equally (or even more) significant to maintain profitability.

In short, this book helps the readers to get clear and straightforward answers to questions such as:

- How to assess whether the business is profitable or not?
- How to manage costs to become profitable faster?
- How to control costs to become more profitable?
- How much should I charge customers?
- How many units of product/service need to be sold to break-even?
- Should I or should I not invest in a given business project?
- How to identify the upfront investments that I need to make?
- How to prepare budgets for business?

The book starts with an explanation of key concepts related to costs and revenues, how they influence the margins of a business and, ultimately, its profitability.

It also provides some insights on how to establish pricing strategies which, in turn, determine the revenues generated by the firm.

Subsequently, the break-even analysis is adopted to test the economic and financial feasibility of a business, and extensive examples of how this method can be applied to testing a business model are presented.

Towards the end, the book introduces techniques that are useful to define a cash-based budget which then can be used to anticipate cash flows of the business as well as to determine funding gaps and needs.

It also provides a practical checklist of actions that a business owner should look at before establishing and committing money into a business venture.

We are hopeful that the readers will find the time spent reading and thinking about the concepts explored in this book to be worthwhile. We wish you the best of reading and the best of luck in your venture!

If you want to keep updated with other publications in this collection, please visit our website (www.startup-finance.co.uk) and drop us an e-mail to receive updates.

Wish you all the best,

Nuno and Bibek

Pathways to a Profitable Business

As a useful start, let us discuss some aspects related to profitability and why it is so important. Any organisation, regardless of its intent to generate profit or not, needs to be managed in such a way that at least it makes enough revenue to be able to pay for its costs.

The sources of revenue can vary depending on the type of organisation, and whether it is profit-oriented or not.

For a public-sector organisation, such as a public service, hospital or university, most of the revenues are generated by public funding, and secondarily by user fees;

For a charity or any other kind of non-governmental organisation, the income would come from a mix of public funding, private donations and user fees;

For a business, most of the revenue is generated by selling its products and services to the market/paying customers.

This book is focused on profit-oriented organisations; however, the same principles can be applied to other types of organisations as well because the rationale in the decision-making process is similar.

Profitability is the primary goal of a business due to the following principal reasons:

- A profitable business tends to be sustainable in the long term;
- A profitable business generates returns to pay for the initial investments made, hence allowing investors to recover the capital employed in the business;
- A profitable business generates profits that can be paid to the shareholders (owners), managers, and employees thereby increasing their commitment towards working and supporting the firm;

- A profitable business enables the firm to invest in its future growth and depend less on other sources of money such as lenders or external investors.

Profitability can be measured by subtracting the costs (of resources used and consumed) from the revenues generated by the business activities. Hence, to be profitable, a business must create a surplus, or a positive difference when costs are subtracted from revenues.

The profitability of a business can be checked from the income statement, which is a summary statement of revenues and costs during a defined accounting period (usually one year).

Accounting techniques can frequently create biases in analysing the profitability of a business, and transform a profitable business into a non-profitable business, and vice-versa.

For example, a company would undoubtedly have closing stocks at the end of an accounting period, and important question would be:

- How to find out the worth of the closing stocks?
- Do we take the market price or the price we paid to acquire such stocks or do we use some other techniques?

These choices obviously will affect the profitability of the firm in the income statement.

Such technical issues might sound complicated, and therefore this book deliberately deviates away from discussing such technical and intricate matters because we aim to present the relevant problems straightforwardly to make it accessible to a wide range of readers.

Therefore, our approach to understanding profitability will be through the analysis of operational profits, which in turn refers to the difference between operating revenues and costs (i.e., revenues and costs related to the usual business activity).

It must be noted at the outset that profitability should not be mistaken with liquidity or the availability of cash: a business may be profitable according to its income statement but may not have enough money available to meet its immediate obligations.

By definition, a firm is profitable if it can generate surpluses from its operational activities, therefore creating a gain on top of the costs needed to support its operations.

In simple mathematical terms, profit can be represented as follows:

$$Profit = Total\ Revenue - Total\ Costs$$

There are two key aspects to this equation, namely, revenue and cost. To generate profit, a business must generate revenue; and to increase its profitability in absolute terms, it needs to maximise the positive difference between revenues and costs.

It is paramount to keep costs under control because costs tend to increase as sales increase. Therefore, the costs must be managed so that they do not grow at a faster pace than sales; otherwise, the benefits of generating more revenues would not compensate for the costs of resources needed to attain them.

Otherwise, the consequence would be an unsustainable revenue growth trajectory which could endanger the future of the business.

Understanding Costs, Revenues and Margins

Understanding the concepts of costs, revenues and margins are crucial to manage any business effectively.

In this book, we will make an extensive use of these concepts, therefore, we start with an in-depth explanation of their meanings and how they will be used throughout the analysis and examples provided.

What are costs

Cost can have multiple meanings depending on the context. Hence, it is usual for the term cost to be preceded by another associated term; for example, direct costs, indirect costs, fixed costs, variable costs, etc.

Cost, in a narrow sense, can be defined as the money spent by a firm to generate operating revenue.

A firm may need to pay wages and utility bills which are easily recognisable as costs, whereas other costs like depreciation may not be so evident because firms would not usually 'pay' for depreciation.

At first, it is essential to understand the difference between direct costs and indirect costs.

Direct costs are those costs that can be exclusively and accurately traced to a particular cost object.

Cost object in this sense refers to any activity of interest for which cost needs to be measured: it could be a product, a service, a mix of products, or a business division, and so forth.

For example, if business owners are interested in measuring the cost of a product that the business produces - such as a simple T-Shirt (cost object) - the fabric needed to make it can be considered a direct cost.

However, the rent paid for the premises where the factory is located would be difficult to assign to the production of T-Shirts accurately if the firm manufactures other clothing items as well.

Hence, the rent in such cases would be an indirect cost as far as the manufacturing cost of the T-Shirts is concerned.

While calculating the manufacturing cost of the cost object, such indirect costs also have to be allocated to the cost object reasonably.

Let us try to illustrate another concept of costs by explaining the difference between direct costs and indirect costs. Imagine that two items have been purchased for the business on a given day: a writing pad (for $2) and a laptop (for $500), both probably having a similar physical size.

The writing pad is not expected to last long, and it will probably be used up within the accounting period of one year.

Hence, the money paid for the writing pad ($2) is both a cost and an expense (money paid out) and can simultaneously be considered a cost for the accounting period.

What this means in accounting terms is that while calculating profit for the period, the $2 will have to be subtracted from the revenue (along with so many other costs) to arrive at the profit figure for that particular period [Remember, Total Profit = Total Revenue – Total Cost].

Examples of other operational costs that are also costs in the same accounting period are wages, labour taxes, social insurance, insurances, utilities, office or vehicle rents, and supplies of any operating raw materials or services.

On the other hand, the laptop can be reasonably expected to last at least a few years; hence, more than one full accounting period.

Therefore, it would be unfair (and against accounting principles) to try to subtract the full $500 from the revenue of the year in which it was bought because the utility of the laptop extends well beyond one year.

Hence, the $500 paid for the computer is an expense but not a cost related to the accounting period (year) in which it was bought, but rather an investment.

If the computer is expected to last for five years (assumption), then it would be prudent to subtract just one fifth or $100 (=$500÷5) from the total revenue for the year so that the economic cost of the laptop can be spread over its five-year life.

The amount of $100 which is subtracted from the yearly revenue (for five years) to arrive at the profit figure is called the depreciation charge, though no actual annual cash outflow of $100 takes place as the equipment had already been paid for.

Even though the business does not pay this $100 as depreciation expenses, such depreciation charges should be assigned to the cost objects when assessing, for example, the production costs of the business.

Regarding how the level of activity influences costs, they can also be divided into fixed or variable costs.

Fixed costs

Fixed costs tend to remain generally the same in the short term (for example one year) whereas variable costs tend to change with the level of output (such as sales). In the following section, we will discuss these differences further.

Fixed costs tend to remain the same regardless of the firm's output which can be measured regarding the number of units produced, as well as the number of units sold (which can be considered as a proxy to a cost object).

That is precisely why fixed costs are so significant because a firm cannot avoid them and, therefore, the business needs to generate enough sales volume to pay for them.

Fixed costs are also generally difficult to assign to products or services, especially if the firm produces more than one product or line of service.

For example, if a Bed & Breakfast (B&B) business is offering night accommodation, laundry services, and restaurant services to customers, it is difficult to pinpoint precisely how much of the rent cost is associated with each of those three lines of services.

Hence, fixed costs are also referred to as indirect costs or overheads.

More importantly, fixed costs are recurrent: incurred every week, month, or year.

Besides, fixed costs are not dependent on having a certain number of customers or the level of goods or services being produced or sold. This means that the firm still has to pay the rent even if it does not manage to sell anything!

All businesses have fixed costs no matter how small or big they are. Below are some examples:

- Accounting and legal fees
- Bank fees
- Sales and marketing
- Travelling
- Insurances
- Office supplies
- Rent of the premises
- Foreseeable repair and maintenance
- Utilities
- Interests
- Salaries and wages

Fixed costs are usually dependent on the installed capacity of the business regarding its maximum output; therefore, it is contingent upon a given operational level.

Installed capacity refers to the maximum production capacity such as the number of units that can be produced by the business during a specific period (usually one year), or the number of units sold.

A decision to increase capacity in response to demand fluctuations, whether permanently or temporarily, could make the firm incur higher fixed costs.

Let us look at the example of a B&B operating with ten rooms on rented premises. The firm has to pay for the same rent per calendar month regardless of the occupancy of the rooms.

However, if a decision is made to expand the business into twenty rooms by renting additional space, the fixed cost (rent in this case) will, in principle, increase.

The same applies if, instead of renting extra space, the business expands its premises by building additional rooms.

Over and above this investment, other costs will be incurred to run the day to day activity of the company, as extra rooms will mean extra costs related to cleaning, insurance, and utilities.

Variable costs

As the term itself suggests, variable costs vary depending on the output of a business; this means that such costs tend to rise as production or sales (or both) increase, and tend to decrease conversely.

Opposite to fixed costs, variable costs can usually be linked to the units of outputs and, therefore, are considered as direct costs. Below are some examples of variable costs:

- Sales commissions paid to agents
- Direct materials and direct labour

- Production supplies for the manufacturing of goods
- Electricity, gas and water consumed (beyond minimum, recurring base charges)
- Extraordinary repair and maintenance costs

For example, in the case of a B&B business in which the output could be measured by the number of rooms sold per day, selling more rooms accrues higher variable costs due to higher consumption of utilities (such as electricity and gas), amenities, or breakfasts served.

Additionally, some costs can be described as semi-variable costs or semi-fixed costs, also known as a semi-fixed cost. These are composed of a mixture of fixed and variable components; hence they are fixed for a set level of output and become variable after the threshold is exceeded.

A typical example would be that of a mobile phone contract where a fixed amount of fee needs to be paid each month as long as monthly allowance is not exceeded; but the consumer would have to pay extra if they exceed the monthly allowance of call time or data and this additional payment depends on the level of excess services used by the consumer.

Cost structure

Classifying a cost as fixed or variable is determined based on whether or not it fluctuates with the volume of output (which can be measured by the number of units produced or sold).

If the cost increases when the output increases, then it is a variable cost; whereas if it remains constant regardless of the change in output, then it is a fixed cost. It is, therefore, critical to know how the costs change as sales increase or decrease.

The total costs of running a business for a given period is the sum of total fixed costs and total variable costs.

Hence, the total cost structure can be mathematically represented as follows:

The following chart illustrates how total costs, i.e. combined fixed cost and variable cost, vary depending on the output:

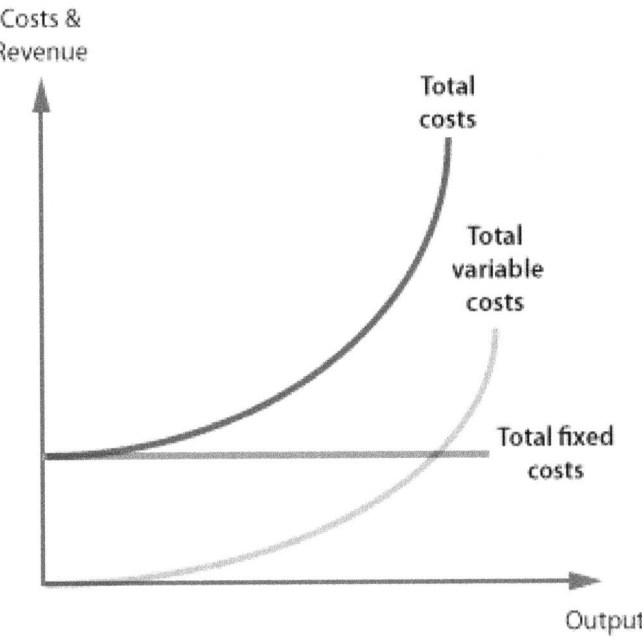

Therefore, it is always imperative to reflect on the cost structure before starting up or expanding a business.

Different businesses have different cost structures which makes it very difficult to identify the correct amount of costs that can be considered healthy. This is why the break-even analysis which will be developed ahead can be useful.

However, as a rule of thumb, it is essential to consider that the higher the fixed costs, the worse for the business: the consequence of high fixed costs is that the company will have to pay for them regardless of having sales or not.

On the other hand, the higher the variable costs mean that the business will only incur on them if and when sales are generated.

Notwithstanding the importance of managing the costs structure throughout all the stages of the business growth, it is particularly important to pay attention to this at the start of the business when availability of initial funds available may be limited as compared to an ongoing established business.

Therefore, it should be considered beforehand if the firm has enough cash ahead to cover the fixed costs for the first year at least; otherwise, it could cause severe problems such as disruption of the business activities in the short-term.

Fixed and variable costs per unit

Fixed costs are relatively easy to forecast as they are more likely to be known in advance, whereas variable costs can be more difficult to anticipate as they can be less predictable and more challenging to measure.

After all, variable costs depend on the volume of the output which in turn depends upon many other factors.

For example, changing the number of units produced by a business can influence the quantity and costs of materials consumed, as well as extra hours of labour needed.

From a practical perspective, it can be difficult to estimate the variable costs per unit of output.

Here are some concrete examples: in a B&B business, the unit of output is associated with the number of rooms sold per day, but could also be the number of breakfasts served; in the case of a company that produces and sells board games, the board game itself is a unit of output.

Let us now move on with a new example.

The GAME Company produces board games and anticipates that the yearly fixed costs are $200,000 and that the firm plans to produce at its peak capacity of 100,000 units (board games).

Even though total fixed costs do not change, the amount of fixed costs per unit tends to decrease with the increase in the number of units produced; i.e., the more units of board games produced, the less the fixed costs per unit.

For example:

Total fixed costs	Production (number of units)	Fixed costs per unit
$200,000	10	$20,000
$200,000	100	$2,000
$200,000	500	$400

However, the variable costs per unit produced remains the same. For example, let us consider that the company has a variable cost of $5 to produce one board game (which includes the cost of the board, box, darts, and cards).

The variable cost per unit remains the same, but the total variable cost depends on the number of units produced, as illustrated below:

Variable costs per unit	Production (number of units)	Total variable costs
$5	10	$50
$5	100	$500
$5	500	$2,500

Therefore, the total fixed cost remains constant but the fixed cost per unit changes with the variation regarding the units of production, and the variable cost per unit remains constant but the total variable cost changes with the number of units produced.

In reality, the unit variable cost may also decrease with the increase in production as a buyer will be able to command a better price at more favourable terms from the supplier; but we will ignore such issues for the sake of simplicity.

What are revenues

Revenues can be defined as the income generated from the sale of goods or services (or any other use of capital or assets) associated with the main operations of an organisation before any costs or expenses are deducted.

Therefore, revenues are the positive income that a business gets from selling products or services and such revenues will be used to offset the total costs incurred so that profit can be generated.

Customers might quite regularly buy goods on credit; such sales are still considered revenue even though cash may have not yet been received.

For simplicity, however, we will assume that all transactions are in cash; i.e. no sales are left unpaid.

Total revenues are calculated by multiplying the number of units of output sold by the price per unit (which is paid by the customer):

Total Revenues = Number of Units Sold × Price per Unit

Forecasting revenues pose at least two challenges: first, we do not have a crystal ball to anticipate the number of units of product or service that will be sold (we will come back to this later); second, we also do not know what the selling price would be for the products. Let us now focus on the issue related to pricing.

Pricing

Pricing is related to setting the rate at which a unit of a product (or service) will be sold. It is far more complicated than it may seem because its determination largely depends on various issues including:

- what the customers are willing to pay for;
- the benefit that customers expect to derive from buying it;
- the marketing strategy of the firm;
- the intrinsic characteristics and value added by the product or service;
- the prices offered by competitors, and so on.

It is also worthwhile, at this point, to distinguish between price-setting firms and price-taking firms.

A price setter is a firm that - as the name suggests - can set the price of one or some of its products to some extent in the market regardless of how the competitors have set the price.

These will be the firms that have highly customised and differentiated products and or are market leaders. Not all businesses can become market leaders and price setters (like Apple or Samsung).

For example, in starting up a coffee house offering purely organic products and no other company nearby offering such organic coffee, the firm can be a price setter to some extent.

On the other hand, firms that have to accept the price set by the market are the price takers. Smaller firms operating within an industry already dominated by other players tend to be the price-takers.

As noted at the beginning of this book, the price of a product should exceed all the costs; but by how much?

Even though pricing can be considered a marketing decision, the price of a product is highly influenced by many factors that the firm does not have control over.

Consequently, products and services should be sold at a rate so that the sales revenues are enough to cover all the fixed and variable costs, while at the same time, providing a satisfactory level of profit.

Therefore, the critical questions are how to assign a price to a product or service:

- Should the price be the same across all geographies and demographic characteristics of the customers?
- Should the price be based on the actual cost of production or based on what the potential buyers would be willing to pay?
- Should the price be the same throughout the whole life cycle of the product?

To simplify our discussion on this matter, we will use three pricing principles that can be a good starting point for pricing decisions.

Cost-based or mark-up pricing

The price is determined by adding a profit element or mark-up on top of the cost of making the product or delivering a service:

$$Selling\ Price = Cost\ of\ Production + Mark\text{-}up$$

An advantage of this approach is that the business will know that its costs are being covered.

However, a key disadvantage is that cost-plus pricing may lead to products being priced above what the customers are willing to pay for.

Below is an example of mark-up pricing, where a business wishes to make a $50 of profit on top of the cost of production per unit:

$$Selling\ Price = \$100 + \$100 \times 50\% = \$150$$

As noted, the difficulty arising from this method is on what the mark-up percentage should be which largely depends on the competitive prices in the market and whether the resulting price would be acceptable to customers.

In the above example, a mark-up of 50% was assumed arbitrarily.

However, how high or low should the mark-up be?

Before deciding on the mark-up, various factors and strategies need to be considered. These issues are discussed in the remainder of this chapter.

Market-based pricing

This relates to the pricing of new products and price is determined by the anticipation of what the customers may be willing to pay for a given product or service.

As a rule of thumb, if the business is into a highly competitive market and does not bring a lot of value or novelty to the market, the customers will not be willing to pay more for the product or service.

This means that the company may have to squeeze down the prices to enter the market which can be referred to as penetration pricing whereby a business sets a relatively low initial entry price to attract new customers and to penetrate the market. This strategy aims to encourage customers to switch to the new product because of the lower price.

However, one disadvantage being that consumers may not like it when the firm subsequently attempts to raise the selling price.

Conversely, if the firm is launching a new product or service for which there is little or no competition (in a somewhat monopolistic setting), it may set a high price before other competitors come into the market.

This strategy is commonly known as price skimming.

Unfortunately, this strategy is difficult to maintain for a long-term mainly because competitors will try to launch rival products or services that will put downward pressure on the price.

It may also dampen demand initially as many consumers would not be able to afford it.

Further, when a product can command a high price in the market, it provides a signal to competitors that there may be plenty of opportunity for making a profit, thus encouraging more competitors to enter the market.

Competitor-based pricing

This approach is mostly dependent on the number of competitors on the market. If there is a strong existing competition on the market, customers are faced with a wide choice of whom to buy from.

Most firms in a competitive market do not have sufficient power to be able to set prices above their competitors.

Therefore, they tend to set prices that are in line with the rates charged by their direct competitors.

However, as the business objective is to maximise profits, companies should look for ways to differentiate their products from that of their competitors; for example, providing better quality, better service, faster delivery or a combination of all of these might distinguish a business from its competitors thus enabling the firm to set a higher price.

An effective pricing strategy reflects a combination of all of the above techniques: prices are capped by what the market is willing to pay for a good or service; should be aligned with competition after considering any differentiation that may exist; and should always cover the costs of producing the product or service.

The pricing strategies should be dependent on the short-term and long-term objectives of the business.

Pricing strategies for the short-term

In the short term (at the stage when the busy enters the market with a new product or service), the prices may have to be lowered to such a level as to attract customers even if that means incurring losses (by not generating enough sales to cover the actual costs).

Of course, such a strategy is not feasible in the long term but might be considered reasonable in the short term if surviving allows the business to take a successful path in the future.

In the short-term, both price-takers and price-setters can take into consideration the incremental cost of production and sales.

Let us look at a concrete example of a Chinese takeaway business: a Monday afternoon can be considered an idle period where the business hardly gets any orders, but the costs related to the chef, rent and other overheads still have to be paid for.

The selling price can reflect the incremental cost of preparing an order. If a customer orders a particular meal that incurs a cost of $3.15 for direct materials (like noodles, eggs, prawns, spices, electricity, and oil), the meal should not be sold for less than $3.15 no matter how idle the business is (unless there is a clear strategy to incur losses just to get a foothold in the market).

So let us assume that the business sells a particular meal for $3.65 on Monday afternoons, which is lower than the normal rate of $7.00.

The direct costs are still being covered (cost of the direct materials needed to produce the takeaway) but the extra margin of $0.50 (=$3.65–$3.15), though partially offsetting other indirect costs might not be able to fully cover the fixed overheads like the rent and the wages for the staff members.

Nevertheless, this is better than no business at all.

However, to be able to pursue this strategy, the business also needs to have spare capacity - such as in the said example - and this pricing should be an exception rather than the norm.

Pricing strategies for the long-term

In the long term, price-setting firms can either use the cost-plus pricing approach or target-costing approach.

As discussed earlier, the cost-plus approach involves figuring out all the costs required to produce goods and then adding a required level of profit margin on top of that to arrive at the selling price of the products.

Price-setting firms can also employ target-costing approach where the target selling price is determined first and then the determined profit margin is deducted from the target selling price.

Whatever remains should be able to cover all the estimated cost of production; if not, costs have to be brought down, or the product will have to be abandoned.

The target-costing approach is adopted at the planning and design phase before actually deciding whether or not to produce the goods. Target costing is mainly suited for non-customized products with expected sales at high volumes.

As it is vital to be aware of some of the pricing strategies that are employed in the business world, let us discuss four common pricing policies:

Promotional pricing - This strategy can take a variety of forms. It might consist of the familiar 'Save $5; was $20, now $15' sales offer.

It could also involve offering some (but not all) products at an unusually low price hoping that customers attracted by such low prices in some products would buy other regularly-priced items as well.

Think of an imaginary situation where a pub lowers the price of its burgers from $5 to 'just $2.50' during certain hours.

Customers attracted by the low price on this one item might be tempted to buy several other food and drink items in the pub.

Moreover, the regular seasonal offers like Boxing Day or Black Friday can also be categorised as promotional pricing.

Differential pricing - This strategy involves setting different prices for the same product in various market segments.

For multiple reasons, manufacturers might decide to charge a lower price for an item ordered over the internet compared to in-store sales; technology-savvy shoppers might find a better deal online for the same product with the use of discount codes while regular shoppers may have to pay the full price even while purchasing the same item through the same medium.

For this strategy to be effective, there should be distinct market segments reacting differently to prices.

Psychological pricing - This strategy is mainly employed in consumer products where customers' purchasing habits can be expected to be influenced, to some extent, by their emotions rather than economic factors.

A conventional example of this kind of pricing is where a product may be priced at $49.99 rather than $50.00 thus giving the impression that the product is much cheaper than it is.

There can also be a situation where someone bought two pairs of jeans for the advertised price of $49.99 whereas she only needed one pair which would have cost her $34.99.

Alternatively, it could also be a case of Buy One Get One Free offer, where a customer pays $49.99 for one pair of jeans and gets the other pair for 'free'.

Products, which usually complement each other, can also be bundled together and offered at a lower price if bought together.

Another approach to psychological pricing could be where the rate of a product is unchanged from the previous year, but the quantity is gradually reduced thus giving the false impression that the price has remained the same from the previous year.

Product-line pricing - This strategy relates to pricing of various products within a product line. The product line, in this case, refers to multiple products that are closely related together.

For example, as an online retailer of laptops, a customer might consider laptops along with mice, or laptop bags within the same product line. If a business is selling printers, the printer itself and the ink cartridges might be considered to be within the same product line.

A strategy often employed consists of selling printers at a low price but later charging more for the ink cartridges that need to be replaced regularly.

Readers might also be familiar with situations where customers get a phone for 'free' if they pay a certain amount monthly for talk time and data.

The above discussion, of course, does not provide an exhaustive list or review of pricing methods and strategies. However, being aware of various pricing techniques and policies would be invaluable to a new business to adjust pricing strategies accordingly.

What are margins

The margin is the difference between the selling price of a product or service and all the costs of producing it.

Hence, margins are the operational profits or losses generated before any interest has been received or paid, any depreciation of assets have been considered, or any taxes on gains have been paid.

The following table illustrates a simplified version of a profit and loss forecast statement of the GAME Company (which produces board games) to demonstrate how this information can be analysed to evaluate the profitability of the business:

	Value
Number of units/games sold (@ $20 per unit)	50,000
Total revenues	$1,000,000
(–) Total variable costs (@ $5 per unit)	$250,000
(=) Variable margin	$750,000
(–) Total fixed costs	$200,000
(=) Operating margin	**$550,000**

The company sells 50,000 units per year at a selling price per unit of $20 (total revenues $1,000,000).

The variable cost of producing each game is $5; hence the total variable cost equals $250,000 (=50,000×$5).

Subtracting the total variable cost from the total revenues gives us the variable margin, which means that after paying for the cost of producing the games the firm will still have $750,000 left to pay for its fixed costs. Hence,

Variable Margin = Total Revenues – Total Variable Costs

Considering that the fixed costs equal $200,000 per year, subtracting this fixed amount from the variable margin results in $550,000 of operating margin, which in this case is a profit.

Hence,

Operating Margin = Variable margin – Total Fixed Costs

However, this will not be the profit available to be distributed to the shareholders of the firm, as other costs (e.g. interest payables, taxes and depreciation) will have to be deducted before the remainder can be considered as profits available to owners.

We can also calculate the variable margin per unit sold, which is called the contribution margin per unit sold:

Contribution Margin per Unit = Selling Price per Unit – Variable Cost per Unit

The contribution margin per unit represents the portion of sales revenue that is not consumed by producing and selling one unit and contributes towards the coverage of the fixed cost of the company.

In the above example, the contribution margin per unit equals $15 which is obtained by subtracting the variable cost per unit ($5) from the selling price per unit ($20).

In other words, each board game that is sold contributes $15 towards paying the fixed costs of the firm; resulting margin equals $15 (=$20–$5).

Testing the business feasibility

We are now in a position to calculate the break-even point (BEP) of the business, which is the point at which cost and revenues are equal, and there is neither profit nor loss. This is also known as the Cost-Volume-Profit analysis.

In other words, the BEP refers to the minimum number of units of output required to be sold to have nil operating profits.

The firm will break-even when it generates enough revenue to cover its overall variable and fixed costs incurred in the course of producing and selling the products or services.

If the business sells the bare minimum units of products to meet these objectives (i.e. reaches the BEP), it will just break-even but will not earn a profit (however, and importantly will not make a loss either).

If the business exceeds the BEP, it will be able to generate an operational profit.

Calculating the break-even point

The calculation of the BEP may be performed using two formulas. The first formula provides the result regarding the number of units of output that need to be produced (quantity) and sold to pay for the fixed costs.

The second formula calculates the BEP concerning the sales volume or revenues (in $ or any other currency).

First, BEP is calculated regarding the number of units.

The result is obtained by dividing the total fixed costs by the contribution margin per unit:

BEP (in units) = Total Fixed Costs ÷ Contribution Margin per Unit

Returning to the example of the GAME Company:

BEP = $200,000 ÷ $15 = 13,333(33) units

With a contribution margin of $15 per game sold, the BEP is achieved at 13,333(33) or roughly 13,333 games: upon the production and sale of 13,333 games, all fixed expenses will be paid for, and the company will report a net profit or loss of $0.

This result is easy to confirm, as follows:

	Value
Number of units sold	13,333(33)
Total revenues (@ $20 per unit)	$266,666(66)
(–) Total variable costs (@ $5 per unit)	$66,66(66)
(=) Variable margin	$200,000
(–) Total fixed costs	$200,000
(=) Operating margin	**$0**

Please note that for calculation purposes we have used 13,333.33 units produced although that will be physically impossible to achieve: 13,333 will be more realistic instead.

Alternatively, the BEP concerning sales volume can be calculated dividing the total fixed costs by the contribution margin ratio; where the contribution margin ratio is the contribution margin per unit ($5) divided by the sale price per unit ($20), thus resulting in the BEP sales volume of $266.660.

Let us also use the case of the B&B to demonstrate this. However, first, we work on some initial assumptions about this business: the fixed cost to run a ten-room business is $100,000 per year; each room is sold per day for $50, and the variable costs per room/day are estimated to be $5.

Thus, the contribution margin ratio, which is obtained by dividing the contribution margin per room/day by the selling price per unit is 0.9 (=$45÷$50).

Therefore, the BEP is:

BEP (in sales volume) = $100,000 ÷ 0.9 = $111,111(11)

These results suggest that we need to generate revenues of at least $111,111 for the year to break-even in this business. If we divide this by the average selling price per room/day (which is $50), the break-even regarding the number of rooms is 2,222(22) rooms over the whole year.

Following is an illustration that visually demonstrates the BEP. On the vertical axis, the volume of sales is represented (in $), whereas on the horizontal axis the output regarding units sold.

The total costs line (C) results from adding the fixed costs - horizontal line starting at B - to the variable costs (which increase proportionally to the increase in the output). The total costs intercept the revenues line (A) at the BEP (P), where the business accrues no losses or profits.

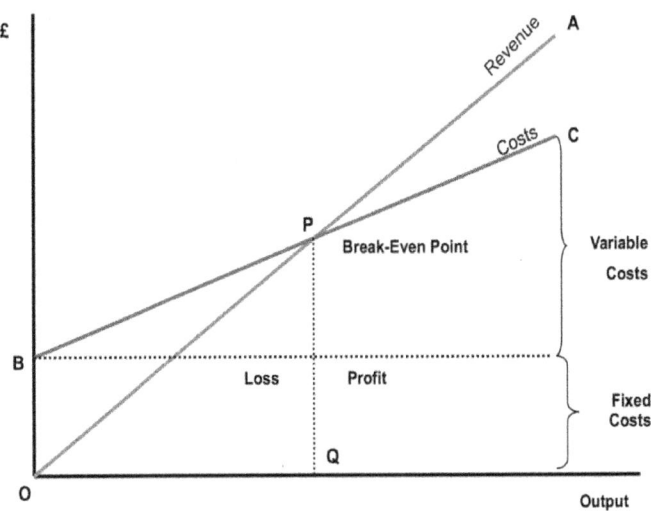

In practical terms, these results also mean that if the firm would not be able to reach the BEP (minimum sales threshold) and cover for all the variable and fixed costs incurred on, it will run out of cash.

Nonetheless, the firms may rely on obtaining additional funds to cover for their needs, such as a loan or an additional investment made by the shareholders as well as acquiring new investors.

Simulating different scenarios

The advantage of the break-even analysis is that it immediately provides an accurate perspective on the minimum volume of sales that needs to be generated.

To be profitable, the firm needs to sell above the BEP; the more quantity, the better.

Therefore, upon knowing these results, one can immediately question the feasibility of achieving the BEP as well as look for ways to surpass them and generate a profit.

However, first, it is useful to ponder how firms could manage to lower the BEP, as it could benefit the cost structure of the firm and reduce its exposure to risks, namely the fluctuation of demand.

To do so, and deriving from the calculation we have done earlier, three variables can be changed to simulate different scenarios that will result in either increasing or decreasing of the BEP:

- fixed costs,
- selling price per unit, and
- variable cost per unit.

Let us now analyse the impact on the BEP if each of these variables is changed.

Going back to the GAME Company, let us first estimate the impact on the BEP by reducing the fixed costs by 20%.

The resulting fixed costs would be $160,000 (=$200,000– 20%×$200,000).

Therefore,

$$BEP = \$160,000 \div \$15 = 10,666(67) \text{ units}$$

Hence, the BEP is reduced compared to the initial situation (13,333 units).

The rationale is that if fixed costs are reduced, the contribution margin that needs to be generated to pay for the fixed costs is also reduced, therefore putting less pressures on the objectives.

Conversely, increasing the fixed costs would push the BEP up, thereby driving the firm to expand its targets.

Now let us try some simulations to see what would happen to the BEP if we maintain the initial fixed costs but increase the selling price per unit, let us say, by 20%.

The resulting new selling price per unit would be $24 (=$20+20%×$20).

$$BEP = \$200,000 \div (\$24 - \$5) = 10,526 \text{ units}$$

As expected the BEP has decreased compared to the initial situation (13,333 units).

The rationale is that if the contribution margin per unit increases as a result of increasing the selling price per unit, each unit sold contributes more towards covering the fixed costs; hence fewer units need to be sold to cover the fixed costs.

Conversely, reducing the selling price would have the opposite effect and raise the BEP.

Now let us see what would happen to the BEP if we maintain the initial fixed costs and selling price per unit, but manage to reduce the variable costs per unit by 20%.

The resulting variable cost per unit would be $4 (=$5–20%×$5).

$$BEP = \$200,000 \div (\$20 - \$4) = 12{,}500 \text{ units}$$

As expected the BEP has decreased compared to the initial situation (13,333 units).

The rationale is that if the contribution margin per unit increases as a result of reducing the variable cost per unit, each unit sold contributes more towards covering the fixed costs; hence fewer units need to be sold to cover the fixed costs.

Conversely, increasing the variable cost per unit would have the opposite effect and raise the BEP.

The results are summarised as follows:

Fixed costs	Selling price per unit	Variable costs per unit
Increase ⇒ BEP increases	Increase ⇒ Contribution Margin increases ⇒ BEP decreases	Increase ⇒ Contribution Margin decreases ⇒ BEP increases
Decrease ⇒ BEP decreases	Decrease ⇒ Contribution Margin decreases ⇒ BEP increases	Decreases ⇒ Contribution Margin increases ⇒ BEP decreases

As noted, the power of break-even analysis is that it immediately allows us to test the feasibility of the sales objectives while also allowing us to simulate different scenarios.

In doing so, we can explore whether it would be feasible to change some factors within the limits of what can be achieved given the constraints of resources, the business model, and strategies.

However, the analysis presented is also fundamental as it enables a better understanding on whether the sales objectives are within reach through reasonable efforts, given the constraints imposed by the initial capacity of the company as well as the market size.

Now, let us expand our discussion on BEP to understand how it can be useful to test the internal capacity of a business.

Testing the operational capacity

Calculating the BEP can be very helpful to determine whether capacity adjustments have to be made to the company.

As we will see, using this method will also be useful in that it may alert us to some pitfalls related to the business planning, particularly to circumstances of under-capacity.

Let us look at the example of the B&B business which has an anticipated capacity of ten rooms which are available 365 days per year.

The expected fixed costs of the B&B are $100,000 per year. The capacity regarding the number of available rooms per year is estimated at 365 days×10 rooms=3,650 rooms per year.

The BEP concerning the number of rooms per year is:

$$BEP = \$100,000 \div (\$50 - \$5) = 2,222(22) \text{ rooms per year}$$

Dividing the BEP by twelve months' results in 185.18 rooms/month. Subsequently, dividing it by thirty (average number of days per calendar month) results in 6.17 rooms/day, which means that it is within the operating capacity of the B&B (which has the capacity of ten rooms per day). The occupancy ratio at the BEP is calculated by dividing 6.17 rooms by ten rooms resulting in 61.7%.

It could be the case that the fixed costs of running the business were estimated at a lower level. Let us see what could happen if, for example, the estimated fixed costs would be $200,000 instead of $100,000.

$$BEP = \$200,000 \div (\$50 - \$5) = 4,444(44) \ rooms/year$$

Dividing this by twelve months' results in 370.37 rooms/month. Subsequently, dividing it by thirty results in 12.34 rooms/day, which means that it is 23.40% above the operating and physical capacity of the B&B which has just ten rooms.

Therefore, decisions would have to be made about how to make this economically feasible.

We assume that, in principle, there would not be much margin of manoeuvre to change either the selling price which is capped by the competition, or the variable costs per room which refers to the minimum necessary costs relating to cleaning, utilities and toiletries while providing a service that meets the requirements of the customers.

Therefore, the most likely options at this stage would be either to attempt to reduce the fixed costs or to increase the capacity of the B&B and expand it to more than 12 rooms.

Hence, this could result in additional risks for the business and is probably not the best decision to be made, at this stage. At least not before testing other alternatives.

A way to overcoming this difficulty would be to identify the maximum amount of fixed costs the business could incur to have a BEP not exceeding the initial capacity of ten rooms per day.

However, acknowledging this means that the company would have to operate at full capacity - which is highly unlikely - but it serves the purpose of explaining how to make this calculation.

We will now return to the BEP formula regarding units:

BEP (in units) = Total Fixed Costs ÷ Contribution Margin per Unit

So, we replace the BEP by the maximum capacity of the B&B which is 3,650 rooms per year, as well as the contribution margin per unit by $45. Therefore,

3,650 room days per year [= 10 rooms/day × 365] = Total Fixed Costs ÷ $45

For simplification, we replace the variable which we what to find (Total Fixed Costs) by X. Solving the equation for X we get

$$X = 3,650 × \$45 = \$164,250$$

The result means that to be able to keep the business afloat, the fixed costs structure should not be above $164,250 per year.

However, this result should be considered the absolute maximum for fixed costs because we have done the calculation based on full occupancy throughout the year, which is highly unlikely.

Let us now assume that realistically the B&B would be able to reach only 50% of its maximum capacity as the average occupancy rate throughout the year, and recalculate the maximum amount of fixed costs:

1,825 room days per year [= 5 rooms/day × 365] = Total Fixed Costs ÷ $45

which is equivalent to

$$X = 1,825 × \$45 = \$82,125$$

This means that realistically the firm should keep the annual fixed costs lower than $82,125 in order to minimise risks. This is based on the pessimistic assumption that the occupancy rate will be only 50%.

However, should the firm assume that the occupancy rate is going to be higher than 50%, the fixed costs can be allowed to increase; but at any rate, the fixed cost should not be allowed to exceed the $164,250 level because this figure was based on 100% occupancy.

Calculating the BEP with multiple products

So far, the BEP has been calculated for a single-product business.

However, firms may be selling more than one product or service. It becomes a bit trickier to calculate the BEP under such circumstances because the different products might have different contribution margins (and a different allocation of fixed costs).

Hence, the following example illustrates how the break-even analysis can be useful when a firm sells more than one product.

For example, the GAME Company could sell a portfolio of two different board games targeted at different users, with different tastes, or of different age groups.

There are two approaches to calculating the BEP in such cases where we have more than one product.

The first one is more basic but faster, and it suggests that we should split the fixed costs for the different products.

The following results summarise the calculation of the BEP for both of the games (Game A and Game B) on a 50/50 cost-sharing basis.

Recalling that total fixed costs for the GAME Company were $200,000 per year,

BEP Game A = $100,000 ÷ ($20 − $5) = 6,666(66) games/year

BEP Game B = $100,000 ÷ ($20 − $5) = 6,666(66) games/year

However, from a realistic perspective, this does not make much sense as probably the different games will use the resources of the firm differently, therefore consuming a different proportion of the fixed costs.

Moreover, the selling prices and variable costs of producing each game may also differ (unlike in the previous example).

A reasonable approach to overcome these difficulties could be to split the fixed costs in such a way that it would reflect the different relative consumption of resources for each product, such as hours of direct labour, and materials consumed.

Other criteria could be used such as the percentage of sales estimated for each product, or the usage of the production space (in square meters) for each type of products game, and so on.

Therefore, we could distribute the fixed costs between both games, based on, for example, on the percentage of their respective sales to the total revenues: for instance, Game A would be allocated 20% of the fixed costs totalling $40,000, whereas Game B would be assigned the remaining 80% at $160,000.

We can also change the assumptions for the selling prices and variable costs of each game: let us assume that Game A has a selling price and variable cost per unit of $20 and $5 respectively, whereas Game B would have a selling price and variable cost per unit of $25 and $15 respectively.

BEP Game A = $40,000 ÷ ($20 – $5) = 2,666(67) games/year

BEP Game B = $160,000 ÷ ($25 – $15) = 16,000 games/year

An alternative way to calculate the BEP for the product mix would be to calculate it by weighting the contribution margin for each game with the percentage used to split the fixed costs between them, as follows:

BEP (aggregated) = $200,000 ÷ ($15 × 20% + $10 × 80%) = 18,181 (81) units

As this result is an aggregated BEP, we would need to split it between the two products. To do so, we multiply the result by the percentage of sales of each product.

Therefore, we obtain a BEP of 3,636(36) for Game A (=18,181(81) × 20%), and 14,545 (45) for Game B (=18,181 (81) × 80%).

Defining profitability objectives

Until now, we have used break-even analysis to allow us to answer a fundamental question:

How many units of product or service need to be sold to break-even and to make a nil profit?

However, the nature of any business activity is to generate a profit and so another critical question is raised:

What sales volume needs to be achieved to make the business profitable?

There are at least two different techniques can be adopted to calculate this. The first is very simple as all we need to do is to add the fixed costs structure to the amount of profit that we intend to generate.

To illustrate the first technique, a slight modification can be made to the existing formula as follows:

BEP (in units) = (Total Fixed Costs + Profit) ÷ Contribution Margin

The result will give us the excess sales (in units) that have to be made to achieve such an objective.

Going back to the B&B, the initial BEP was estimated to be achieved by selling 2,222(22) rooms in a year. However, this means a nil profit after the operating costs have been accounted for.

Now, let us assume that the management had the objective of achieving a profit of $15,000 for the first year of trade.

One way to estimate how this would impact the sales objectives is by adding this required profit amount to the fixed costs and recalculating the BEP:

$$BEP = (\$100,000 + \$15,000) \div \$45 = 2,555(55) \text{ units}$$

Hence, the difference between this and the previous BEP would be an additional 333 rooms that need to be sold to achieve that profit for the year.

An alternative technique would be to use the operating margin formula, which we have shown previously, as follows:

Operating Margin = Total Revenues – Total Variable Costs – Total Fixed Costs

Recall that operating margin is zero at the BEP by definition because there is no profit or loss. So, the above formula essentially becomes:

0 = Total Revenues – Total Variable Costs – Total Fixed Costs

Now, if we want to make some amount of profit, we can modify the above formula as follows:

0 + Profit = Total Revenues – Total Variable costs – Total Fixed costs

The preceding formula can be rewritten as:

0 + Profit = (Number of Units Sold × Selling Price per Unit) – (Number of Units Sold × Variable Costs per Unit) – Total Fixed Costs

Which is equivalent to:

0 + Profit = Number of Units Sold × (Selling Price per Unit – Variable Costs per Unit) – Total Fixed Costs

Which is equivalent to:

Profit = (Number of Units Sold × Contribution Margin per Unit) – Total Fixed Costs

Now, our aim here is to find out the number of units to sell so that we can make a profit of $15,000. Let that number of units to be sold be Y.

Considering that our contribution margin per unit is $45 and the total fixed cost is $100,000, the above equation can be expressed as:

$$\$15,000 = (Y \times \$45) - \$100,000 \Rightarrow \quad \$15,000 + \$100,000 = (Y \times \$45) \Rightarrow$$

$$\$115,000 = Y \times \$45 \Rightarrow \quad Y = \$115,000 \div \$45 = 2,555(55) \text{ units}$$

Hence, to earn the required profit of $15,000, the firm has to produce and sell 2,556 units. This result from the second approach is the same result as the first approach shown above.

Further examples of how to apply the break-even analysis

This section aims to provide further examples and clarifications on how the break-even analysis can be used in planning a start-up business.

Specifically, two examples are discussed to demonstrate the applicability of the break-even analysis in two different businesses: service-oriented business and product-related business.

The aim of this section is to make it easier to understand how the break-even analysis can be used in either case with the same simplicity and effectiveness.

Example 1 - Counselling practice

This example specifically refers to a counselling practice, but it could also be applied to any freelance practice in the health sector, or other sectors such as accounting, web design or computer programming.

Therefore, the example provided should be used as a guideline that can be easily adopted by anyone starting a similar venture.

The business will have only one employee, the founder. An office will be rented to attend to customers and conduct the therapy sessions.

The therapy sessions will be carried out on the premises so there would be no additional travelling to meet customers in other locations. The unit of output is considered to be a one-hour session of therapy.

First, let us identify the fixed costs relating to establishing such a practice. Whenever costs are paid on an annual basis (such as insurance, professional membership fees, etc.), we divide the figure by 12 to allow for a monthly estimation.

Fixed costs	Monthly value
Accounting and legal fees	$65
Insurances	$20
Sales and marketing	$50
Rent of the premises	$500
Office supplies	$45
Salaries and wages	$2,280
Total	**$2,960**

To estimate the variable costs, we need to identify the costs that could be directly connected to each one-hour session. If providing this service entails travelling to visit a customer, then the associated costs should be considered as variable costs.

In this example, let us assume that the direct variable costs associated with a one-hour therapy session would be as follows:

Variable costs	Per unit
Printing of materials to support the therapy	$1
Essential oils needed for the treatment	$2
Total	**$3**

The price charged by the therapist per hour is $50. To calculate the BEP, we will use the formulas previously described, as follows:

> *Contribution Margin = Selling Price per Unit – Variable Costs per Unit*

Hence,

> *Contribution Margin = $50 – $3 = $47*

And to determine the BEP:

> *BEP = Total Fixed Costs ÷ Contribution Margin*

Hence,

> *BEP = $2,960 ÷ $47 = 62.98 sessions per month (one hour each)*

To facilitate the analysis, the figure is rounded up to the nearest integer value, namely 63 sessions.

The result means that to pay for the fixed costs, the counsellor needs to fill 63 one-hour sessions, which will turnover approximately $3,150 per month (=63×$50).

From an operational perspective, 63 sessions per month would represent an average of 15.75 sessions per week (considering four weeks per calendar month) and 3.15 sessions per day (assuming five working days per week), which is feasible for such a business in its early stages.

We will discuss the applicability of the break-even analysis for an online retailer in the following section.

Example 2 - Online retailer

This example relates explicitly to the establishment of an online company that sells fashion jewellery but it could also be applied to any practice that trades goods either online or in a retail shop.

Therefore, the example provided should be used as a guideline which can help with the implementation of a methodology that can be easily used by anyone involved in a similar venture.

In this example, the self-employed founder will be the only employee. The unit of output is one order which includes one item of jewellery (e.g. earrings, bracelet, necklace, or ring).

The company plans to offer a catalogue of approximately 500 different items of jewellery and an average stock of 20 units of each, meaning that the overall stock will be around 10,000 units.

The stock is imported to the UK from China. The cost range including taxes is between $1 and $2 per item, with an average price of $1.50 per item. The pieces are stocked in the UK and dispatched to customers internationally.

One small warehouse will be rented to stock and prepare the dispatching of orders. The company will replenish its stock as appropriate considering the sales accomplished.

The selling price is established by applying a 700% mark-up to the purchase price, meaning that on average the selling price per item will be $10.5 (=$1.50×7), excluding postage.

This price is within the range that is accepted in the market for similar goods sold online in the UK.

For simplification purposes, no taxes such as VAT will be considered in this example.

All the sales are generated online through the company's website as well as by using third-party e-commerce platforms such as eBay and Amazon.

It is estimated that, in the beginning, 99% of the sales will be generated through these third channels, which charge an average of 20% commission (applied to the selling price) on every purchase.

It is also estimated that 90% of the sales will be generated in the UK and only 10% overseas.

First, let us identify the fixed costs relating to the establishment of such a business. As previously mentioned, whenever costs are paid on an annual basis, we divide the figure by 12 to allow for a monthly estimation.

Fixed costs	Monthly value
Rent of the premises	$500
Office supplies	$60
Insurances	$20
Sales and marketing	$50
Accounting and legal fees	$65
Salaries and wages	$2,230
Total	**$2,925**

To estimate the variable costs per unit, we now need to identify the direct costs of each different item. For break-even analysis, this would be very time-consuming, and it would not bring much value to a high-level approach which is the one we intend to use this methodology for.

Therefore, the assumption that will be applied to this example is to consider the average costs per item as being $1.50 and the average selling price per unit to be $10.50.

Therefore, the average cost per item would be 14.29% (=$1.5÷$10.5) of the selling price.

In this example, let us assume that the direct variable costs associated with one sale would be as follows:

Variable costs	Per unit
Purchase cost per item	$1.50
Commission per sale (20% of the selling price)	$2.10
Packaging per item sold	$1.20
Postage per item sold	$0.80
Total	**$5.60**

To calculate the BEP, we will use the formulas previously described, as follows:

Contribution Margin = Selling Price per Unit – Variable Costs per Unit

Hence,

Contribution Margin = $10.50 – $5.60 = $4.90

And considering that

BEP (in units) = Total Fixed Costs ÷ Contribution Margin

Hence,

BEP = $2,925 ÷ $4.90 = 596.94 items per month

To facilitate our analysis, we will round the figure to the nearest integer value, namely 597 items. From an operational perspective, 597 items per month would represent an average of 19.9 (or 20) items per day (assuming 30 days/month on average).

Achieving this result would probably not be very feasible in the beginning, but it is within what is expected to be achievable in the medium term as the company gains online presence and enhances its reputation.

How to build a budget

In the previous section, we focussed mainly on break-even analysis which provides clear operational targets to be achieved to avoid losses for a business.

However, a company also needs detailed plans to coordinate different functions (like production, marketing, sales, or recruitment) within the business so that the operation is smooth and profitable.

Implementing a budgeting process can be of help in the planning process, and this is what will be discussed in this chapter.

What is a budget

The word budget is heard on numerous occasions:

the government talks about the budget almost every year which invariably leads to arguments and counterarguments among politicians and economists;

the local authority might declare that they cannot do the repairs on the road due to lack of budget;

consumers might be complaining that they cannot buy that new gadget because it is not within their budget.

A budget in all of these contexts is related to the expected costs and income for a given period.

However, budgeting is not just about forecasting costs; it is also about projecting various other aspects of a business-like marketing, recruitment, production volume, and so on.

Therefore, it helps not just with planning but can also be useful for controlling operations and evaluating performance, among other things.

Why do businesses need a budget?

Let us go back to the example of GAME Company with anticipated sales of 40,000 games in December. Imagine the disruption to the operation if the business ran out of the required materials to produce the games just before that peak month.

Alternatively, imagine that the necessary materials are there but not enough workforce to package the games during the period of high demand!

These are some of the situations a business should try to avoid, by careful planning ahead.

Different types of budget

There are different types of budgets like production budget, sales budget, cash budget, and so on.

With so many different budgets, which budget is the better one to start with first?

The budget begins with the critical factor which is generally the sales (i.e. the money that the business plans to generate by selling products or services).

Hence, it is the Sales Budget that needs to be prepared first and then other budgets like material purchase budget, advertising budget can follow, based on the sales' budget.

Preparing a sales budget requires an expected number of sales at the estimated selling price for a given period.

Now, if we had a crystal ball that would be easy!

Right after this section, we will discuss the challenges of forecasting sales and provide some discussion on how to mitigate those challenges.

Thereafter, we will continue our discussion on budgets starting with the sales forecast.

Forecasting sales

As previously discussed, an important aspect of budgeting is related to anticipate the sales of the units of output of the products or services which will be sold.

This is highly complex, as few techniques will allow to forecasting sales with accuracy, particularly when launching a new business in which there is no history or record of previous sales.

However, some guidelines can be used to establish a reasonable estimate of the number of units that can be potentially sold on the market.

Quantify the market in which the firm is entering

Market quantification can be a daunting and expensive process requiring money and time.

Assuming that new businesses do not have plenty of either, they may have to resort to using secondary data sources such as newspaper articles, academic journals, public reports, statistics, and market research studies made by credible organisations.

Market quantification implies working out a number of potential of customers, either individuals or businesses that could be potential buyers of the services or products sold by the firm.

This number represents the maximum number of customers, implying that all the competitors entering the same market will share them.

Unfortunately, a common mistake made by start-ups and growing businesses is aiming for an unrealistic number of target customers, and this can destroy any credibility on their business plans.

The advantage of market quantification is that having done so makes it unlikely that the business will forecast sales quantities that are much larger than the market it intends to serve in the first place.

Therefore, quantifying the market will require searching online with keywords related to the characteristics of the target individual customers, such as their gender, social habits, or economic power.

In quantifying business consumers, other features may be relevant such as the sector of activity, the number of workers, or the amount of revenues.

As a rule of thumb, relying on only one source of information is not recommended. It would be more prudent to confront the data by comparing different sources; this is because there are likely to be differences among various sources.

The objective of this approach is to get an estimate of the potential market size, and not an exact or precise dimension as this will be almost impossible to accomplish.

As an example, let us assume that the GAME Company has identified that the total market size in the UK for board games is 500,000 potential buyers per year. Naturally, the firm will not attain a 100% market share at the start as there are other competitors already on the market; therefore, it is reasonable to estimate a much lower percentage at the entry stage.

The next table exemplifies how different market shares can be simulated for different scenarios depending upon how optimistic or pessimistic the firm is.

Market size estimate (UK)	Potential market share	Number of units sold
	1%	5,000
500,000 individual buyers	5%	25,000
	10%	50,000

Identify the maximum output capacity of the firm

This approach deals with the identification of the internal capacity of the business regarding how many units of product or service could be produced given a certain level of initial capacity to start.

The capacity can be expanded or reduced over time but, as noted previously, higher capacity could mean higher fixed costs.

Therefore, it is advisable to consider setting up a reasonable capacity that minimises fixed costs and consider the possibility to scale it up later if and when the market demand grows.

A good strategy at the market-entry stage when firms are unsure of how the market will react would be to consider outsourcing the production (entirely or partially) to other firms.

In doing so the business would probably end up paying more for the production which would increase its variable costs, however, the fixed costs structure would be kept at minimum levels, therefore reducing the risks.

However, this is a strategic and challenging decision to be made as it is not always possible to outsource the production to third parties, either because there are none that can provide the same standards of quality, the price (and variable costs) may be too high to bear; or just because the firm does not trust another partner to handover knowledge and expertise which may be critical for the business.

Firms should be able to have a rough estimate on what the sales volumes of their competitors are. If a competitor is a public company, various data along with financial reports should be available publicly.

However, for those firms which are not public, they may not have the same level of requirement to make their data available to the public. In such cases, one can either make a direct observation of such competitors by accessing publicly available data on their website - which could be relevant if the business is online.

As noted, anticipating sales requires a considerable amount of research and also establishing assumptions to move on with it, as there is not a single best technique that will provide accurate information.

Overall, the idea is to get a rough estimate of the market size so that the firm will be able to understand whether its output capacity is adequate, and the sales forecasts are in line with the market size, the current level of demand, and anticipated levels of demand for the near future.

Once the firm enters the market, it will be able to identify whether the forecasts are too optimistic or pessimistic and make the necessary adjustments.

As the company gains some track record concerning sales, for example after one year of activity, it will be in a better position to establish a sales forecast for the forthcoming year.

The learning process, market knowledge and acumen gained will be already there and will prove to be invaluable inputs for making further projections.

However, even after having gained some record of accomplishment, it would be prudent for firms to perform market analysis on a regular basis such as monthly or quarterly using at least the techniques discussed above.

Ultimately the learning results from the previous chapter related to the break-even analysis should also be considered as a test and support for the decision-making process on what concerns sales forecasts.

Master budget

The master budget comprises different sub-budgets which are interlinked, and altogether allows a better understanding of the various inputs that the firm needs to mobilise in advance and to meet the sales objectives.

Let us start with forecasting the sales for the GAME Company.

Based on the previous findings, the GAME Company expects to attain a 10% market share during the first year, therefore, being able to sell in the region of 50,000 units.

Accordingly, they have prepared an annual budget which can be broken down into four quarters. We will work on the budget for the last quarter of the year, ending on the 31st of December 201X.

	Oct	Nov	Dec
Expected Sales (in units)	2,000	3,000	10,000

For simplicity, we assume that selling price per unit will remain at $20 for the foreseeable future; this allows us to prepare a sales budget in monetary terms pretty easily.

We multiply each month's expected sales in units with the expected sales price ($20) to come up with the Sales Budget as follows:

	Oct	Nov	Dec
Expected sales (in units)	2,000	3,000	10,000
Selling price per unit ($)	$20	$20	$20
Expected sales ($)	$40,000	$60,000	$200,000

To ensure smooth supply to the customers and to avoid missing sales targets due to insufficient stock, the company might decide to hold about 20% of the following month's sales as a reserve.

This information allows us to calculate the monthly Production Budget, as follows:

	Oct	Nov	Dec
Expected sales (in units)	2,000	3,000	10,000
(+) Required closing stock (in units)	600	2,000	0
(=) Total stock needs	2,600	5,000	10,000
(–) Opening stock	100	600	2,000
(=) Production units	2,500	4,400	8,000

The above budget shows that, for the month of October, 2,500 units of products need to be produced (even though the expected sales is only 2,000 units).

This is because, on top of the required units of 2,000 for October, an additional 600 units are needed (20% of November's requirement of 3,000) as safety reserve for the following month.

The same applies for November and December. We will assume that the closing stock of December is nil as after the peak season (Christmas) the sales are expected to drop sharply for the following months; we will also assume that the opening balance for October (i.e. closing balance for September) is 100.

However, there are also 100 stock units in the opening balance from September (closing balance for September is the opening balance for October).

Hence, there is a need to produce 2,500 units (=2,000+600–100) in September. The same applies for November and December.

A natural progression from this point forward would be to estimate the direct materials to purchase in the future to keep up with the production.

Let us assume that the firm needs 1.2 Kg of materials (which would include all materials including plastics, cardboard, cards, and packaging) to produce one unit of the final product ready for delivery.

To avoid any disruption in supplies, let us consider that the firm keeps 20% of the following month's production requirement in stock.

For the month of October, we will assume that the opening balance (i.e. closing balance from September) is 370 Kg.

We can now prepare a material Purchase Budget for the quarter.

	Oct	Nov	Dec
Production units	2,500	4,400	8,000
Materials needed (Kg)	3,000	5,280	9,600
(+) Required closing stock (Kg)	1,056	1,920	0
(=) Total materials needed (Kg)	4,056	7,200	9,600
(–) Opening stock (Kg)	370	1,056	1,920
(=) Materials purchase (Kg)	3,686	6,144	7,680

Now the business has a rough idea of how much materials it needs to buy every month. For example, during the month of November, the firm needs to buy 6,144 Kg of materials.

In real life, it will also have a fair idea of how much each Kg of materials is going to cost. To keep things simple, let us assume that each Kg of materials cost $2.20.

This allows us to figure out the amount of money that would be needed to buy these materials for each of the coming months. For the month of October, the amount of money required to purchase the necessary materials would be $8,109 (=3,686×$2.20), and so on for other months.

	Oct	Nov	Dec
Materials purchase (Kg)	3,686	6,144	7,680
Materials purchase ($)	8,109	13,517	16,896

Taking a step further, now let us assume that direct labour needed to prepare one board game is six minutes.

This is to say that one individual would have to work for six minutes (0.1 hours) to make one board ready for selling.

If the semi-skilled worker needs to be paid $12 per hour, it is possible to figure out how many labour hours would be needed for production purpose and the cost of such labour hours.

This can be done using the Direct Labour Budget as shown below:

	Oct	Nov	Dec
Production units	2,500	4,400	8,000
Required Labour Hours	250	440	800
Direct Labour Cost ($)	3,000	5,280	9,600

Apart from the money needed for the purchase of materials (as worked out in one of the earlier tables), this new information allows us to estimate the additional amount of money needed each month to pay direct wages.

The derived number of labour hours enables us to figure out roughly how many individuals need to be hired during each of the above months.

For instance, assuming that one individual works 150 hours per month, the number of individuals necessary for the month of October is 2 (=250÷150).

Similarly, for the month of November, approximately three individuals would be needed and for the month of December 5 individuals for direct production.

Possessing this information would enable the business owner to estimate the recruitment and training needs.

So far, we have taken into account direct costs (i.e. direct materials and direct labour). Let us now account for indirect materials and indirect labour as well.

Let us assume that variable manufacturing overhead is $0.50 (50 pence) per unit produced and the fixed manufacturing overhead is $1,800 per month. This fixed manufacturing overhead would be incurred regardless of the number of products produced (and sold).

Therefore, the Manufacturing Overhead Budget would look like this:

	Oct	Nov	Dec
Production units	2,500	4,400	8,000
Variable manufacturing overhead ($0.5)	1,250	2,200	4,000
(+) Fixed manufacturing overhead ($)	1,800	1,800	1,800
(=) Total manufacturing overheads ($)	3,050	4,000	5,800

We will add one more category of costs to our budget now: selling and administrative. This cost will be based on the sales figure rather than the production units.

If we assume a selling cost of $2.50 per unit sold (for postage and delivery) along with a fixed selling and admin cost of $700 a month to cover for other rubrics, we can easily make the Administrative Budget as follows:

	Oct	Nov	Dec
Sales units	2,000	3,000	10,000
Variable selling & admin ($)	5,000	7,500	25,000
(+) Fixed selling & admin ($)	700	700	700
(=) Total selling & admin ($)	5,700	8,200	25,700

The above table illustrates that total selling and administration expense for the month of the October will be $5,700. Similar estimates are shown for November and December thereby giving the business owners opportunity to plan accordingly.

Cash-based budgeting

A cash budget details a company's cash inflow (money received) and cash outflow (money paid out) during a specified period, such as a month, quarter or year.

Its primary purpose is   to   provide   the   status   of   the company's cash position at any point in time, and it is used to assess whether the business has sufficient money to operate.

Companies use sales forecasts to create a cash budget, along with assumptions about mandatory spending.

If a company does not have enough money to operate either in the long term or short term, it must raise more capital by issuing stock or by taking on debt.

In the case of a start-up or expanding a business, cash-based budget is of utmost relevance for estimating the needs of liquidity.

This is because the firm will not start generating money immediately as it needs to enter the market, promote its offer before having customers, and make sales.

Hence, the firm needs to have a clear idea about operating cash flow, which is a measure of the amount of money generated by a company's normal business operations.

Operating cash flow indicates whether a company can make sufficient positive money flow to maintain and grow its operations; or if it may require external financing for business expansion.

Operating cash flows concentrate on cash inflows and outflows related to the firm's principal business activities, such as selling and purchasing inventory, providing services and paying salaries.

Any investing and financing transactions (e.g. interest on a loan) are excluded from operating cash flows and reported separately, such as borrowing money or making capital expenditures. However, we will address these issues later.

Using the tables that we have prepared so far in the previous section, we are in a position to prepare a cash budget; i.e. a budget that tells us about the cash position of the business.

An important reminder is that this is not a profit/loss account (which we will deal with later).

Assuming that the opening cash balance for October was -$20,000 (i.e. $20,000 into an overdraft), the cash budget would look as follows:

	Oct	Nov	Dec
Opening balance	-$20,000	$141	$29,144
Sales	$40,000	$60,000	$200,000
(–) Less:			
Materials Purchase	$8,109	$13,517	$16,896
Direct Labour	$3,000	$5,280	$9,600
Variable manufacturing overhead	$1,250	$2,200	$4,000
Fixed manufacturing overhead	$1,800	$1,800	$1,800
Selling and admin	$5,700	$8,200	$25,700
(=) Closing balance	$141	$29,144	$171,148

In the above table the cash inflows and outflows for each month are used to determine the month's ending balance, which is the beginning balance for the following month.

This process allows the company to forecast its cash needs throughout the year.

The above projection shows that the business will have more cash available throughout the quarter. So far we have made the predictions in the simplest of settings without taking into account so many complexities that one may have to deal with in real life.

For example:

- Shall we get the full amount of sales revenue in cash?
- Alternatively, how much of that would turn into irrecoverable debt?
- How long will the buyers take to pay the company for the goods supplied?

Let us incorporate the effect of the delay in collecting the cash generated by sales in the previous cash-based budget.

For this purpose, the company forecasts that 80% of the receipts will be collected in the same month as the sale and the other 20% received one month after the sale.

All the other costs are expected to be incurred on in the respective month.

	Oct	Nov	Dec
Opening balance	-$20,000	-$2,859	$22,144
(+) Payment Collection	$37,000	$56,000	$172,000
(=) Cash inflows	$17,000	$53,141	$194,144
(−) Variable costs	$17,359	$28,497	$55,496
(−) Fixed costs	$2,500	$2,500	$2,500
(=) Cash outflows	$19,859	$30,997	$57,996
Closing balance (inflows−outflows)	-$2,859	$22,144	$136,148

In this example, the GAME Company computes the cash inflows by adding the initial cash position (October) to the receivables collected during that month (80% of the sales made), plus the receivables collected from the transactions made in September (20%) which we assume are $5,000.

In this month, as the cash outflows will total $19,859, the company will have a negative cash balance of $2,859 at the end of the month.

This is assumed to be covered by a bank overdraft allowance which the company has previously negotiated and which will incur charges. To simplify the discussion, we will not include these overdraft charges in our analysis.

This negative cash balance will be the initial cash position in October. To compute the cash inflows during that month, the negative cash position will be added to the sales collected that month.

In November, the company will receive in cash $48,000 (=$60,000×80%) plus 20% of the sales generated in October which were not collected in the previous month and represent $8,000 (=$40,000×20%), therefore, totalling $56,000.

Hence, the cash inflows will be -$2,859+$56,000=$53,141. Note that the remaining 20% of the sales made in November will only be collected in December.

The cash outflows in November will be $30,997, which will be subtracted from the inflows resulting in a positive cash balance of $22,144 in that month.

Using the same methodology for the month of December, the company will have a positive cash balance of $136,148.

As noted, there is a big difference at the end of year cash position of the firm according to this example, which is more realistic, as compared to the previous case ($171,148) which did not take into consideration the delay in collecting money from sales.

In practical terms, the firm could also delay its payments to the suppliers for some time, which could significantly ease its cash position.

Depending on the nature of the business, companies need to have cash in advance that will allow them to pay for the operational costs before they can generate any revenues. Such cash balance should be enough to pay for operational expenses and keep the business afloat on its own.

Furthermore, some companies need to spend money upfront to set up the adequate infrastructure and resources that are required in advance of starting the business.

The upfront costs that need to be made only once to establish a business properly are commonly referred to as capital expenditures (or CAPEX).

Therefore, capital expenditures are the funds that a business uses to purchase primary physical goods or services to start or expand the company's abilities to generate profits. They are expected to provide utility to a business for more than one year.

Examples of capital expenditures:

- Buildings
- Land
- Computer equipment
- Office equipment
- Furniture and fixtures
- Machinery
- Vehicles
- Software
- Intangible assets such as patents

To establish a cash budget, the company needs to be able to anticipate the CAPEX and forecast the sales as well as the fixed and variable costs that comprise the operating expenditures (or OPEX).

An operating cost is incurred on buy a business through its normal operations.

These costs generally include the same categories of costs, which we have previously discussed when introducing fixed and variable costs.

As operational costs make up the bulk of a company's regular spending, the management will examine ways of lowering them without causing a critical drop in quality or production output.

With this in mind, let us consider an extended version of the previous example in which the GAME Company had to make an upfront investment of $50,000 in October to market a new game which would be released during the Christmas season.

Considering this CAPEX in the budget helps understanding when the business will make enough cash to be able to pay back the initial investment and start generating a profit.

To do this, we can include the initial investment as a cash outflow in September and run the model with this new element:

	Oct	Nov	Dec
Opening balance	-$20,000	-$52,859	-$27,856
(+) CAPEX	-$50,000	$0	$0
(+) Revenues	$37,000	$56,000	$172,000
(=) Cash inflows	-$33,000	$3,141	$144,144
(–) Variable costs	$17,359	$28,497	$55,496
(–) Fixed costs	$2,500	$2,500	$2,500
(=) Cash outflows	**$19,859**	**$30,997**	**$57,996**
Closing balance (inflows–outflows)	-$52,859	-$27,856	$86,148

As noted, and although the cash position at the end of the year was still favourable, the company accumulated negative cash balances in October and November, until it finally had a positive cash flow in December. The significance of adding the CAPEX investment to the model is that it clearly shows whether the business has the capacity to generate enough cash flow to pay for the upfront costs on top of being able to pay for the operational costs, and most importantly, when the cash flows will become positive.

Profit and loss statement

A Profit and Loss (P&L) statement is a summary statement exhibiting the revenues, costs and costs, and resulting profit (or loss) during a specific period, usually a fiscal quarter or year.

These records provide information about a company's ability - or lack thereof - to generate profit by increasing revenue, reducing costs, or both.

The P&L statement is also referred to as statement of profit and loss, income statement, statement of comprehensive income, statement of financial results, and income and expense statement.

The P&L statement follows a general form, beginning with an entry for revenues, known as the top line, and subtracts the costs of doing business, including the cost of goods sold, operating costs, taxes, interests and depreciation.

After deducting all these costs, what remains is the net income, known as the profit (also referred to as bottom line or earnings).

In this case, we will establish a P&L budget using the assumptions of the previous examples to help in clarifying how this table is made and the main differences between the P&L and cash-based budget. This will be helpful to explore the concept of profitability further.

The P&L statement can be used to measure the past performance of a company as well as to make a budget. The main difference, when compared to the cash-based budget, is that P&L ignores when actual cash inflows and cash outflows occur, but only considers the underlying activities that will lead to the generation of such cash flows.

For example, a company making a sale does not mean that it always collects the money after the transaction has been made. It is standard business practice, particularly between companies, that the seller issues an invoice that is sent to the buyer, who should pay it within an agreed period.

When such invoices are sent out but are yet to be paid, they are referred to as accounts receivables for the firm.

It may be reasonable for such receivables to remain outstanding for a few weeks or even months. In P&L statements, such sales are still included even though the actual money may not have been received by the firm; whereas in a cash-budget, the sales on credit will be ignored because the firm has received no cash for such a credit sale.

Hence from the perspective of P&L analyses, the revenue generated by the sale should be considered in the P&L statement in the same accounting period (e.g. quarter or year) that the sale was made regardless of whether the transaction was on cash or credit; but from the perspective of the cash-based budget, only actual receipts (cash inflow) during the accounting period are considered regardless of when the transaction was made.

The same applies to costs. As companies buy from third parties not only resources such as goods and raw materials but also other services (such as utilities) that they need to support the business activities, they receive invoices from the suppliers that need to be paid.

The firm itself may delay making such payments by weeks or even months for various reasons. Monies owed to others by the firm are generally referred to as account payables, and such payables are still subtracted in P&L statement to arrive at the profit figure.

The invoices are recorded on the month to which the costs were made (or resources consumed).

However, they are recorded in the cash-based budget only and when the costs are paid off by the firm (cash outflow).

To make this understandable here is how a P&L statement could be made using the same information of the previous example:

	Oct	Nov	Dec	Total
Revenues	$37,000	$56,000	$172,000	$265,000
(−) Costs of goods sold	$14,159	$22,797	$32,296	$69,252
(=) Gross profit	$22,841	$33,203	$139,704	$195,748
(−) Other costs	$5,700	$8,200	$25,700	$39,600
(=) Net profit	$17,141	$25,003	$114,004	$156,148

As this is not a cash budget, the initial line is suppressed (initial cash position), for simplification purposes we will assume that the production costs are named as the costs of goods sold.

Subtracting the cost of goods sold from the revenues, we get the gross profit.

After that, we deduct the other fixed and variable costs that are not directly related to the production of the goods (selling and admin) and obtain the net profit.

As noted, at the end of the quarter, the accumulated net profit for the company is $156,148, which is obtained by adding up the net profits for all the months within the accounting period up to that point.

On the other hand, the cash balance at December-end stands at $86,148 only.

In practical terms both these approaches (cash-based budget and P&L) complement each other when analysing the feasibility of a business, and therefore should be used not only to make forecasts but also to measure the performance of the firm against the objectives that were initially envisaged.

Another difference between P&L and cash budget is that the P&L statement also takes into account some non-cash accounting items such as depreciation. Depreciation is considered a cost but actual cash outflows do not occur for depreciation.

For example, a van purchased last year for $10,000 might be worth $8,000 this year and, as such, the depreciation cost for the van for the year would be $2,000; but this money is not paid out to anyone and hence is not an actual cash outflow for the year. However, this discussion is beyond the scope of the current book.

Investment Decisions - to invest or not to invest?

So, let us now imagine that we have thought about our potential business; and have taken steps to estimate the initial investment needed, the yearly sales, various costs, and even profit!

Now, the question we may want to ask is this:

Can the profit that we expect to earn from the business considered to be a reasonable compensation for the risk that we are taking (by investing our wealth)?

Let us suppose that we have $30,000 to invest in a business. The compensation that we want for that investment would depend on the level of risk that the business possesses.

If the reward is adequate we would be happy to invest; otherwise, we would not want to invest. This is as simple as this!

However, how do we define adequate compensation?

Going back to the example of our $30,000, we can invest that money in a virtually risk-free investment like UK government bond and the yearly return (interest) can be expected to be pitiful. We would probably get an annual interest of 1% (or $300).

Though this level of return can be considered minimal, we are sure to get that return, and our investment will never be lost because the UK government can be reasonably expected to pay back the money!

In that sense, the investment is secure, but the return (interest) is probably not that good.

So, if we invest our money in a business, which by definition is going to be riskier compared to the previous scenario, and expect to get a return of

1% per year, it is no good because we could earn that much (1%) by taking no risk at all.

Since we are putting our money on the line by investing, we would need adequate reward to compensate that extra risk being undertaken.

Though figuring out the required rate of return for a rational investor is beyond the scope of this book, we will assume that 15% (per year) is the appropriate compensation that would make us happy for the business risk undertaken.

With this information, we can now formally proceed towards doing calculations on whether or not a business should be conducted from purely monetary and risk perspective.

Now suppose that we have invested the $30,000 into a business, and the net profit we can expect at the end of 1st, 2nd and 3rd year is $9,000, $13,000, and $15,000 respectively.

To keep things simple, let us also assume that the machinery we bought for this business will be obsolete by the end of the 3rd year which means we will have to cough up another $25,000 if we want to continue with the activity.

Based on the riskiness of the business and the possibility that we could lose our investment, we want a 15% return per year as compensation for the risk we are taking. Is the business worth investing?

From a naive perspective, it might seem like a worthwhile investment because we are going to get back a total of $37,000 (=$9,000+$13,000+$15,000), which is more than our initial investment of $30,000.

However, we have not taken into account the time value of money which says that $1 today is worth more than $1 tomorrow. This is because we are expected to earn an interest in our capital.

To illustrate further, another investment option we have is to put the money in the Dodgy Bank that is offering a fixed rate of interest of 15%

per year on a three-year deposit, interests paid annually, and the capital returned at the maturity.

In essence, by depositing the money in this bank, our $30,000 today should be worth $34,500 next year, by adding the initial deposit to $4,500 of interests paid by the bank (=$30,000×15%); which is to say that $30,000 today is worth $34,500 one year from now, or, to put it the other way around, $34,500 one year from now is equal to $30,000 currently (at that specific level of risk).

Now let us look at the pay-outs from the above options:

	Today	Year 1	Year 2	Year 3
New Business Project				
Cash Flows	-$30,000	$9,000	$13,000	$15,000
Present value today of the future cash flows	-$30,000	$7,826	$9,830	$9,863
Net present value	-$2,481			
Dodgy Bank				
Cash Flows	-$30,000	$4,500	$4,500	$34,500
Present value today of the future cash flows	-$30,000	$3,913	$3,403	$22,684
Net present value	$0			

The $9,000 expected one year from now in our proposed investment is worth only $7,826 now!

To put differently, if we deposit $7,826 now at 15% interest in a bank having a similar level of risk, we will get $9,000 back after one year [=$7,826+$1,174 interest (=$7,826×15%)].

The following simple formula can give an easier way of finding the present value of any amount of money:

Net Present Value = Future Value ÷ (1 + required rate) period

where the period is the number of periods (in this case years) after which the cash inflow is expected.

So, for the first cash inflows from the New Project,

Net Present Value = $9,000 ÷ (1 + 15%)1 = $7,826

Similarly, for the second cash inflows,

Net Present Value = $13,000 ÷ (1 + 15%)2 = $9,830

and so on.

If we add all the present values of the expected cash flows and take away the initial investment, we are left with a Net Present Value of -$2,481 (note the negative sign) in the first example.

This is to say that we will be worse off by $2,481 if we invest in that project because the present value of all the future cash flows is less than what we are spending now on that project.

On the other hand, our investment in the bank would yield $4,500 each year in the form of interest, and we will also get our initial deposit of $30,000 at the end three years (hence the final payment of $34,500).

Since our required rate of return was 15% and the bank was paying us exactly 15% interest, the Net Present Value is $0 (and not negative).

If the bank starts paying us more than 15% interest, then the Net Present Value will be positive. Hence, as long as the result is nil or positive, we will not lose money by investing in that project.

For multiple projects of similar risk and investment requirement, we would want to invest in a project with the highest Net Present Value, which in this case would be the bank.

So far, we have assumed that the investment is for three years only.

However, businesses have going concern; that is to say, companies are expected to last indefinitely. As such, the cash inflows are supposed to be indefinite as well.

Therefore, under this circumstance, how do we find the Net Present Value of infinite cash inflows?

So let us modify our earlier proposed project slightly. Instead of projecting that cash flows will stop after Year 3, what if we become more realistic and assume that the business will continue indefinitely and will yield a profit of $3,000 on Year 4 and every year after that?

We might think about selling the company in Year 5, but that should not matter to our calculation because the price we will get for the business when we sell it should theoretically be equal to the present value (at the time of selling) of all future cash flows that can be expected from the business.

Now we have another challenge of finding the present value of hundreds (or thousands or even more) of expected cash flows (due to going concern of the business)!

If we assume that the hundreds of cash flows will be in equal amounts and that our required rate of return remains the same, there is a surprisingly easy way of calculating the present values of all such cash flows.

Present values of indefinite cash flows of equal amount, the first of which starts one period (year) from now can be derived as follows:

Present Value of Indefinite Cash Flows = Cash Flow ÷ Required Rate

To prove this point, let us assume that we deposited our $30,000 in the bank for an indefinite period and will keep on getting interest of $4,500 (at 15%) every year indefinitely.

The present value, of all such cash flows of $4,500, should intuitively be $30,000 because that is what we have deposited in the bank!

Applying the above formula should also give us the same present value of $30,000 (=$4,500÷15%).

Equipped with this knowledge, now we are in a position to find the present value of an indefinite number of equal cash flows that could be expected from a business.

Let us focus again in the earlier modified example, where we assumed that the business would not cease in three years, but rather it would keep on generating $3,000 profit in Year 4 and every year after that.

The cash flows can now be tabulated as follows:

	Today	Year 1	Year 2	Year 3
Cash Flows	-$30,000	$9,000	$13,000	$15,000
Value of indefinite cash flows				$20,000
Total cash flows	-$30,000	$9,000	$13,000	$35,000
Present value today of the future cash flows	-$30,000	$7,826	$9,830	$23,013
Net Present Value	$10,669			

Let us take a closer look at the above table. Value of indefinite yearly cash flows of $3,000 starting from Year 4 and beyond is $20,000 (=$3,000÷15%) in Year 3.

This is to say that if we wanted to sell off this business at the end of the Year 3 (after taking in the 15,000 profit for that year), we would want to sell it for no less than $20,000. Hence, the total cash flows in Year 3 can be restated as $35,000.

We then find the present value of all these cash flows; for example, the present value of $35,000 three years from now is equal to $23,013 [=$35,000 ÷ (1+15%)3].

Adding all the present values and taking away the initial investment, we get a Net Present Value of $10,669.

It is good to know that this is a positive figure now which implies that by investing in this particular project, we would be increasing our wealth by $10,669 immediately.

To put it slightly differently, investing in this project is like paying $30,000 with our left hand and straight away getting $41,669 (=$30,000+$10,669) in our right hand!

We will recap the project appraisal technique in a few steps below:

- The Net Present Value technique starts with projecting the expected cash flows (profits) from a business for all the future periods (years).
- We then calculate the present values of all such cash flows based on time value of money.
- We add all the cash flows and take away the initial investment; what remains is known as the Net Present Value.
- A project with a positive Net Present Value can be undertaken as this enhances the wealth of the investor.
- There are few other similar techniques for evaluating projects; most of them employ the idea of the time value of money.

However, discussing other methods is beyond the scope of this book. Nonetheless, it may be noted that Net Present Value is one of the most important and widely-used techniques of project evaluation.

Bibliography

Brealey, R. A., Myers, S. C., & Marcus, A. J., 2010. Fundamentals of corporate finance 6th ed., Boston: McGraw-Hill/ Irwin.

Drury, C., 2015. Management and cost accounting 9th ed., Andover: Cengage Learning.

Pride, W. M., Hughes, R. J., & Kapoor, J. R., 2016. Foundations of business 5th ed., Boston: Cengage Learning.

Sangster, A. & Wood, F., 2015. Frank Wood's business accounting 1 13th ed., Harlow: Pearson Education.

Warren, C., Reeve, J., & Duchac, J., 2016. Financial & Managerial Accounting 14th ed., Boston: Cengage Learning.

www.ingramcontent.com/pod-product-compliance
Lightning Source LLC
Chambersburg PA
CBHW072203170526
45158CB00004BB/1752